Responsible Pet Care

Parakeets

Responsible Pet Care

Parakeets

TINA HEARNE

Rourke Publications, Inc.
Vero Beach, FL 32964

no hen with a
cobalt parakeet.

© **1989 Rourke Publications, Inc.**

Library of Congress Cataloging-in-Publication Data

Hearne, Tina.
  Parakeets.

  (Responsible Pet Care)
  Includes index.
  Summary: Examines the different varieties
of parakeets and describes how they may
be housed, exercised, handled, fed,
cleaned, and bred.
  1. Budgerigars–Juvenile literature. [1. Parakeets.]
I. Title.
II. Series: Responsible Pet Care
(Vero Beach, Fla.)
SF473.B8H43   1989   636.6'864   88-30609
ISBN 0-86625-182-0

CONTENTS

1   Why Choose A Parakeet?   6

2   Varieties   8

3   Aviaries   10

4   Cages   12

5   Exercise   14

6   Handling   16

7   Feeding   18

8   Cleaning And Grooming   20

9   Breeding   22

10   The Young   24

11   Ailments   26

12   Health And Longevity   28

   Glossary   30

   Index   31

Why Choose A Parakeet?

The parakeet, or budgerigar, is admired for its color and beauty; for its cheerful, friendly nature; and for its hardiness. It is the most popular cage and **aviary** bird in the world.

All pets need some daily attention, but the parakeet needs very little. It is easy and inexpensive to rear. Feeding is simple, since the diet consists mainly of seeds. Keeping cages and aviaries clean is not difficult, particularly because the birds' droppings are small and rather dry. Exercise is easy to organize if a few basic safety rules are followed. Grooming needs very little effort, as the parakeet is usually able to keep itself in good condition.

Social birds such as parakeets are best housed in an aviary. The main advantages are companionship and the opportunity for flight.

The parakeet's diet consists mainly of seeds. This parakeet is eating millet.

Parakeets are best kept in an aviary, where they can fly and live with other parakeets or parrot-like birds such as cockatiels. Because parakeets are sometimes aggressive with timid birds, it is not safe to keep them with canaries.

If you cannot provide an aviary for pet parakeets, they can live in cages. If possible, keep a pair of birds in the same cage for company. If you are able to have only one parakeet, be prepared to offer it lots of attention. Single parakeets respond well to human interest, and some learn to talk if encouraged when they are young. Indeed, some parakeets talk too much!

The parakeet is one of the few pets that can live happily in an apartment. As such, it is a very good choice for the responsible pet owner.

Varieties

All pet parakeets are descended from the wild Australian bird, *Melopsittacus undulatus*. The original parakeets were light green, but many other varieties have now been bred.

Parakeets today fall into one of four color groups: green, yellow, blue, and white. Each group includes three tones, yielding twelve basic varieties of parakeets: light green, dark green, olive green; light yellow, dark yellow, olive yellow; sky blue, cobalt, mauve; white sky blue, white cobalt, white mauve.

Dark-eyed clear yellow parakeet. The brown cere (the skin above the beak) indicates a female, or hen, bird.

Light green parakeets are the color of the original birds caught in the wild, and so are also known as "normals." A variety known as pied banded light green (note the band of yellow across the chest) is seen here with a cobalt parakeet. The blue cere color of each indicates that they are male, or cock, birds.

Three other factors – gray, slate, and violet – alter these basic colors slightly and produce twelve more varieties. In the greens, for example, you will find gray greens, gray dark greens, and gray olive greens.

Pied parakeets are bi-colored. The upper chest may be yellow and the lower chest green. In banded pied parakeets, a blue chest may be divided by a white band across the middle.

Cinnamons and graywings have fainter head and wing markings than normal, and their body color is lighter. The cinnamon parakeet has markings of cinnamon brown; the graywing has markings of light gray. Opaline birds have no markings at all on the **mantle**, which is the area of the back between the wings.

Albino parakeets have also been bred. In the blue and white series, the albinos are white birds with red eyes. In the green and yellow series, the albino variety is a yellow bird with red eyes. It is given the name lutino.

You may also see some rarer varieties, such as the crested parakeets, in photographs.

9

Aviaries

A collection of parakeets is usually kept in an aviary. This is the best possible housing for captive parakeets, which are by nature **social birds**. The company of other birds is important to them, but so too is the opportunity to fly. They also need room to move from perch to perch, to nest, and to breed. No captive bird has much freedom, but the aviary bird has more than most.

Aviaries can be built indoors or out. Wherever it is built, the aviary should be sturdy enough to keep the parakeets secure. Most aviaries are constructed of wire-mesh screens, supported on a timber frame. Portable indoor aviaries can rest on a cabinet or a stand with wheels. Where there is room, indoor aviaries can be large, taking up a whole corner of a room.

A sturdily built, timber-framed aviary. The flooring and the mesh screens of the aviary are securely joined together to stop predators, such as rats, from entering at ground level.

3

Sociable parakeets perch together in an aviary. These birds show a marked preference for high-level perching. Provide plenty of high perches in both the day and night compartments to avoid squabbling over the best positions. Natural perching, as seen here, is best.

Outdoor aviaries must protect parakeets from bad weather and from **predators**, such as rats and raccoons. An outdoor aviary is divided into two parts. The enclosed sleeping quarters must be weatherproof and free of drafts. Unless the climate is very temperate and never dips below freezing, even at night, this enclosure must have a heater. An abundance of high-level perches will prevent squabbling at night, when the birds enter through holes leading from the flight area.

Sometimes parakeets like to sit in the rain, but the flight area is usually partly roofed. Supply a selection of food and water containers and plenty of natural perching in the form of branches. The floor can be concrete or earth, providing predators cannot get in. Nest boxes can be added at breeding time.

Access to outdoor aviaries should be protected by using double entrance doors. If one door is always securely shut before the other is opened, the birds will never be able to escape accidentally.

Cages

One or two parakeets can be housed comfortably in a cage. For companionship, it is best to keep two birds together. The cage should be as big as possible. Sometimes a homemade cage is bigger and better than a commercial one.

Most homemade cages are constructed of timber, with a wire mesh screen at the front. This design makes them more draft free than commercial cages (those purchased from a pet shop or other store). In bad weather, this is an important factor.

Commercial cages are usually made of wire and plastic. The best have horizontal bars for the birds to climb. These cages have the advantage of being easy to wash clean, but are brittle and can easily be broken. They must always be handled carefully.

This lone caged parakeet has a toy companion. Make the parakeet's home environment as interesting as possible, and include some horizontal bars for climbing. The zygodactyl toes (two pointing to the front; two to the rear) are common to all climbing birds such as parrots and woodpeckers.

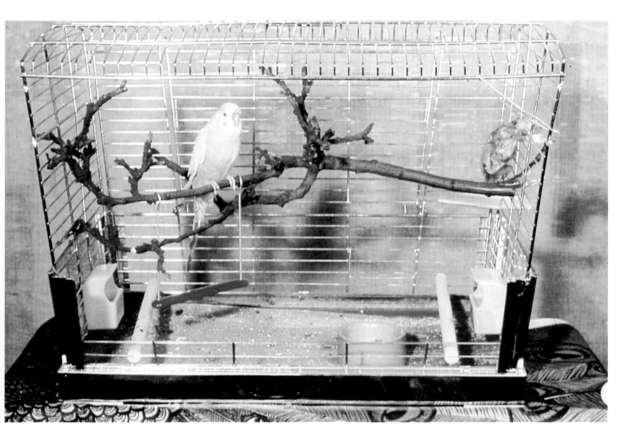

Loneliness and boredom constantly threaten the solitary parakeet. Sensible, safe toys can help to keep the bird occupied and interested. Some time spent out of the cage each day is essential to the happiness of the caged parakeet.

Any cage — commercial or homemade — should be furnished with perches. Branches of varying size make natural perching places. Most commercial cages have thin perches of smooth wood. Perches that are too thin and slippery are hard to hang onto. They can cause a parakeet's claws to become overgrown and its feet to become cramped.

Food and water containers must be accessible to the owner from outside the cage, so they can be cleaned and refilled without opening the cage door. The floor should be covered with a layer of sand or a sandsheet.

Toys, swings, and a mirror can keep a solitary parakeet happy. For this reason, toys serve a useful purpose in the cage. But don't overcrowd the cage with toys — too many will hinder the parakeet's movements.

Where the cage is placed in a home is also important. Parakeets need to live where there is good daylight, but away from drafts and excessive sunshine. Avoid putting the cage directly in front of a window.

13

Exercise

The wild parakeets of Australia fly huge distances. They constantly rove around arid grasslands searching for food and water. Every year the flocks migrate many hundreds of miles to breed in one particular area of Australia. This explains why exercise is so important to captive parakeets.

Aviary birds always have the opportunity for restricted exercise. This is the advantage of housing parakeets in an aviary and the reason the flight area must be as big as possible.

Caged birds are at the mercy of their owner. They have no opportunity to stretch their wings unless the owner lets them out of the cage for a period of exercise each day. Parakeets need this, and every responsible owner must provide it.

A flock of the wild Australian parakeet, Melopsittacus undulatus, descends on a water hole. The wild parakeets fly huge distances over the arid Australian outback, searching for food, water, and suitable breeding places.

In an aviary, the birds have constant opportunity for flight, although very restricted. The flight area should be as big as possible, with good natural perching as shown here.

Make the room as safe as possible before opening the cage door. Give the birds at least half an hour of freedom each day. They often fly only for a short while. Many select a high vantage spot and perch there most of the time. They do little damage, because their rather dry droppings are easily picked up.

At the end of the period, tame parakeets will climb onto your finger or onto a stick held out for them. There is no need to fuss about catching the birds. They will eventually return to their cage for food and water and because it is their own territory. Once daily exercise becomes part of their routine, they get into the habit of returning to the cage afterwards.

Handling

Aviary birds do not usually become very tame. When they need to be handled, they are best caught in a net. In an emergency, any parakeet can be caught by dropping a cloth over it. Another method is to place a hand across the bird's back, with the head between the first and second fingers. Gently restrain the parakeet by closing the thumb and other fingers across the abdomen.

Caged parakeets are often very tame. They get so used to being near their owner that they become **finger tame**. Finger tame birds are so trusting that they will perch on one finger and allow themselves to be carried in that position. These are the easiest birds to return to the cage after exercise.

Finger tame birds are also the ones that may learn to talk. For any kind of success, you must start when the bird is young, from six to eight weeks old. Those that have not learned to talk by the age of six months are not likely to do so. Some people claim that male parakeets, called cocks, are more likely to talk than females, called hens. It is also said that women and children, because of their higher voices, make better teachers than men.

Placing a hand across the bird's back, with the head between the first and second fingers, is one of the proper ways to pick up a parakeet.

Light green and sky blue males perch on the hand. Cage birds may become very tame if they are handled regularly from an early age, and some learn to talk.

Once the parakeet is trained to perch on the finger, lessons can begin. Start with the bird's name. Then teach short words, one at a time. Finally try phrases. Repeat the words many times, and as the birds learn to mimic exactly what they hear, be consistent. Always use the same words and the same tone of voice.

Feeding

The natural food of wild parakeets in Australia is seeding grasses. In captivity, bunches of local seeding grasses, together with a millet spray, can be hung in the cage or aviary. Commercial seed mixtures make up the **staple diet** of pet parakeets. Most mixtures contain canary seed and millet. The best also contain some high quality seeds, such as red rape. Others include artificial seeds that supply additional vitamins and minerals.

The birds do not eat the whole seed. They remove the husk and eat only the kernel of the seed. The husks drop to the floor or back into the feeding bowl. They must always be blown off before refilling the container. A bowl that looks full may contain nothing but empty husks. Some parakeets have starved to death this way.

Gray blue and white sky blue parakeets enjoy seeds, which are their natural food. Good seed mixtures are available in packets and in blocks (rear). Millet sprays (front) are popular and useful at exhausting times such as molting and breeding, but can encourage a parakeet to overeat.

Parakeets like green food, such as lettuce, and some like a section of apple or orange. The main feeding time is early morning.

The Australian parakeets also eat green food. After a sudden shower of rain, they feed on the fresh green plants that quickly germinate. Captive parakeets like green salad vegetables. Some will eat grated carrot; others like a segment of apple or orange.

All seed-eating birds use grit in their digestion. Any parakeet seen pecking at the mortar between bricks or tiles probably lacks grit. Cuttlefish bone is another useful addition. It allows the birds to keep their beaks trim and clean and provides calcium. Similarly, a commercial mineral block should be fixed where the birds can reach to peck at it; it will provide your pet with all the vitamins and minerals it needs to stay healthy.

Finally, fresh drinking water must always be available. Where several birds are kept together, use several drinking bowls.

Cleaning And Grooming

Most cages and aviaries need cleaning thoroughly at least once a week. The frequency will vary according to the size of the cage or aviary, the number of birds held in it, and the amount of time they spend there.

Every cage and aviary needs some daily attention. Each day, blow away the seed husks and wash and refill the food and water bowls. Remove any vegetable matter left over from the previous day and replace it with a fresh supply. Note the condition of the cage or aviary floor and clean it if necessary. The sandsheet in the bottom of a cage may need to be brushed clean, even if it does not need replacing.

As you clean their living quarters, check the condition of the birds. They normally groom themselves, but sometimes they need help. For instance, an aviary bird, with access to the earth, may collect a ball of dried mud under its feet. These balls of earth are very painful and must be softened with water to be removed.

Parakeets need water if they are to groom themselves properly. Aviary birds may perch in the rain for this reason. Here a light green parakeet uses its feet in grooming.

Wild parakeets converge on a water hole in the Australian interior to bathe and drink. Provide water for pet parakeets to drink and to use in grooming. Some like a saucer of water to splash in; others like to be sprayed with water; some will roll in a wet turf.

Parakeets need water for grooming. In an outdoor aviary, birds can sit in the rain. Afterwards they are able to preen their feathers thoroughly. Cage birds can be given water in one of four ways. Most owners simply place a saucer of water in the cage. Others buy a bird bath that clips over the cage entrance. Some owners spray their birds occasionally or put a wet turf in the cage for the parakeets to flutter in. Whichever method you use, make sure the birds' feathers have time to dry before evening.

Breeding

The **cere**, the waxy skin above the beak, is normally blue in a cock bird and brown in a hen. For successful breeding, you will need to keep an equal number of cocks and hens.

In Australia, wild parakeets are not nest builders. They lay their eggs in a hole in a eucalyptus tree. In captivity, your birds will not build a nest. Instead, you must provide nest boxes for them to use. In an aviary, provide more boxes than they will need to allow them some choice of site. Since parakeets like height, position the boxes at the same level to avoid squabbling.

The ideal time of year to provide nest boxes is in the spring, when conditions are best for the young chicks. The birds will be in breeding condition when the cock has a very blue cere, and feeds the hen with **regurgitated food**. A hen in breeding condition will also regurgitate food and will begin to search for a suitable nesting place.

Round parakeet eggs are laid on alternate days and hatch in the same sequence eighteen days later.

A nest box is fixed high in an aviary. Parakeets are very good family birds. During breeding, the cock feeds the hen, and then she feeds the young with regurgitated food. Never remove the cock at breeding time, since the whole clutch depends on him.

A female parakeet usually lays five or six eggs, one every other day. While the female is **incubating** the eggs, the male will feed her. A breeding pair must never be separated.

A good pair will raise as many as three **clutches**, or broods, of baby parakeets a year if the nest box is available. This is hard on the birds and also produces far more young than you can possibly find suitable homes for. Responsible pet owners control the rate of breeding by removing the nest box or by removing eggs as they are laid.

The Young

The incubation period lasts for eighteen days. The young hatch on alternate days in the order the eggs were laid. At this time they are blind and naked. The eyes open on about the sixth day, and by then their feathers are beginning to grow. The tiny birds spend at least four weeks in the nest box and an additional week or two in the aviary or breeding cage. There they are taught how to fly and how to eat hard food.

Very young parakeets should not be disturbed. The hen spends a lot of time inside the nest box with her chicks, keeping them warm by spreading her wings over them. During the time the chicks are in the nest box, the cock feeds the hen who, in turn, feeds the chicks with regurgitated food. In this way, the entire family depends on the cock. Once they begin to leave the nest box, the cock continues to help feed the fledglings, and it is he who teaches them to dehusk seeds.

The young remain in the nest box for a month. By that time their plumage is complete, and they are strong enough to venture outside. They remain dependent on the cock and hen for about six weeks. At that age the young can de-husk seed and are mature enough to be placed in other homes.

Chicks are blind and naked when they hatch, but by the end of the first week their eyes have opened and their feathers begin to grow.

The young chicks are not fully fledged until they are five or six weeks old. At this age they are distinguished by dark bars of color that run across their foreheads. These bars disappear at the time of the first molt, when they are about twelve weeks old.

Parakeets are capable of breeding when they are three or four months old, but they should not be allowed to do so. Wait until they are ten or eleven months old and are stronger. Up to this age, the sexes should be kept apart to prevent the strain of early breeding.

Ailments

Parakeets are prone to infections of the **respiratory tract**: colds, bronchitis, and pneumonia. Isolate a sick bird from others and keep it warm, well away from drafts. Consult a veterinarian immediately. Prompt attention can save a bird's life. Without medication, the bird will gasp for breath, with its beak gaping open and its tail pumping. Eventually it becomes too weak even to perch and will huddle on the floor of the cage.

Another distressing ailment is scaly face. This condition is due to a tiny organism that causes a scaly crust to grow around the beak and eyes and also on the feet and legs. Isolate the parakeet from others, because scaly face is **contagious** and will quickly spread to the other birds. Consult a veterinarian. The organism can be killed off if treated promptly.

Birds remain as healthy as these sky blue and light green parakeet when kept in good conditions. Parakeets seem to thrive best in a warm, dry environment. Those subjected to cold and drafts may succumb to respiratory tract infections such as colds, bronchitis, and pneumonia.

When many parakeets are kept together, there is a danger of disease spreading among them. For this reason, isolate a sick bird at the first sign of illness.

Parakeets can usually, but not always, trim their own beaks and claws, providing they have access to natural perching and cuttlefish bone. Overgrown claws may have to be trimmed with pet nail clippers. Cut straight across the claw, removing only the overgrown tip. Be careful not to cut into the blood supply.

Sometimes the upper or lower **mandible** of the beak is overgrown. These conditions are known as overshot beak and undershot beak and are **congenital defects**. In other words, the parakeet was born that way. A veterinarian may be able to correct the fault by regular trimming.

Birds sometimes begin plucking out their own feathers. Feather plucking is a sign of distress, usually caused by boredom. This habit is difficult to stop, but improving the bird's environment — perhaps by introducing another bird for company — may help.

Health And Longevity

Parakeets bought from a reliable pet shop or bred from healthy stock are likely to have a life span of five to ten years. Eight years is common; twelve years or more is unusual but not unknown.

Healthy parakeets spend a lot of time quietly perching, but they are alert to all that goes on around them. During periods of great activity they will fly about, feed, bathe, perform acrobatics, talk, or sing noisily, but they remain quiet much of the time. A parakeet in good health will perch effortlessly without wobbling, with the body held well clear of the branch. The normal breathing is fast but quiet, and the beak remains closed. The eyes are bright and clear, and the **third eyelid** does not show. The **vent** is clean, and there is no sign of diarrhea.

A parakeet such as this cobalt cock, kept in ideal conditions, should live eight years or longer.

28

In cold weather a parakeet may fluff out its feathers to insulate its body from low temperatures.

In the healthy bird, the feathers are well preened and rest close to the body. In cold weather, they may be fluffed out to insulate the bird from low temperatures. The long tail feathers normally molt twice a year.

A good environment is vital. Responsible pet owners keep their birds in clean, dry conditions. They feed them good quality seed, especially when the birds are molting or breeding. Such owners are the ones most likely to have their birds a long time. In return, the parakeets will give years of companionship, interest, and pleasure.

GLOSSARY

Aviary   A large enclosed area for keeping birds.

Cere   The waxy skin at the top of a bird's beak.

Clutches   Groups, or broods, of baby birds.

Congenital defects   Imperfections that birds or animals are born with.

Contagious   Catching; a contagious disease can be transmitted from one animal or bird to another.

Finger tame   Tame enough to perch on one's finger.

Incubating   Keeping eggs warm so they will hatch.

Mandible   The upper or lower part of a bird's beak.

Mantle   The area of a bird's back between its wings.

Predators   Animals that prey on other animals for food.

Regurgitated food   Partly digested food that is brought back into the mouth.

Respiratory tract   The system that helps a bird or animal to breathe.

Social birds   Birds that like the company of other birds, animals, or humans.

Staple diet   The main kind of food.

Third eyelid   An extra eyelid that many animals and birds have to protect their eyes.

Vent   An opening for passing waste foods.

INDEX

Aviaries 6, 7, 10-11, 14, 16, 18, 20, 21, 22, 24

Bathing 21, 28
Beaks 19, 22, 26, 27, 28
Breeding 10, 11, 22, 23, 25, 29

Cages 6, 7, 12-13, 14, 15, 16, 17, 18, 20, 21, 24, 26
Chicks 22, 24, 25
Claws 13, 27
Cleaning 12, 20-21
Color 6, 8-9

Diet 6, 18

Eggs 23, 24
Exercise 6, 14, 15, 16
Eyes 9, 24, 28

Feathers 21, 24, 27, 29
Feeding 6, 18-19
Feet 13, 20, 26
Flight area 11, 14
Flying 6, 10, 15, 24, 28
Food 13, 14, 15, 18, 19, 20, 22, 24

Grooming 6, 20-21

Handling 16-17
Health 28, 29

Infections 26

Life span 28

Melopsittacus undulatus 8
Molting 25, 29

Nest boxes 11, 22, 23, 24
Nesting 10, 22

Perches 10, 11, 13, 27
Pet shops 12, 28

Scaly face 26
Seeds 6, 18, 19, 20, 24, 29
Sleeping quarters 11

Talking 7, 16-17
Toys 13

Varieties 8-9
Veterinarians 26, 27

Water 13, 14, 15, 19, 20, 21
Wings 9, 14, 24

We would like to thank and acknowledge the following people for the use of their photographs and transparencies:

Cover	Hans Reinhard/Bruce Coleman Ltd
Title Page	Hans Reinhard/Bruce Coleman Ltd
P. 6/7	Sally Anne Thompson/RSPCA
P. 8/9	Dennis Avon/Ardea London Ltd Hans Reinhard/Bruce Coleman Ltd
P. 10/11	Sally Anne Thompson/RSPCA
P. 12/13	Hans Reinhard/Bruce Coleman Ltd Sally Anne Thompson/RSPCA
P. 14/15	Bruce Coleman Ltd Hans Reinhard/Bruce Coleman Ltd
P. 16/17	Sally Anne Thompson/RSPCA Hans Reinhard/Bruce Coleman Ltd
P. 18/19	Hans Reinhard/Bruce Coleman Ltd Aquila Photographics Ltd
P. 20/21	Jane Burton/Bruce Coleman Ltd V Serventy/Bruce Coleman Ltd
P. 22/23	Aquila Photographics Ltd
P. 24/25	Aquila Photographics Ltd
P. 26/27	Hans Reinhard/Bruce Coleman Ltd
P. 28/29	Dennis Avon/Ardea London Ltd Hans Reinhard/Bruce Coleman Ltd